Parent's Introduction

We Both Read is the first series of books designed to invite parents and children to share the reading of a story by taking turns reading aloud. This "shared reading" innovation, which was developed with reading education specialists, invites parents to read the more complex text and story line on the left-hand pages. Then, children can be encouraged to read the right-hand pages, which feature text written for a specific early reading level.

Reading aloud is one of the most important activities parents can share with their child to assist them in their reading development. However, *We Both Read* goes beyond reading *to* a child and allows parents to share the reading *with* a child. *We Both Read* is so powerful and effective because it combines two key elements in learning: "modeling" (the parent reads) and "doing" (the child reads). The result is not only faster reading development for the child, but a much more enjoyable and enriching experience for both!

You may find it helpful to read the entire book aloud yourself the first time, then invite your child to participate in the second reading. In some books, a few more difficult words will first be introduced in the parent's text, distinguished with **bold lettering**. Pointing out, and even discussing, these words will help familiarize your child with them and help to build your child's vocabulary. Also, note that a "talking parent" icon ⭗ precedes the parent's text, and a "talking child" icon ⭗ precedes the child's text.

We encourage you to share and interact with your child as you read the book together. If your child is having difficulty, you might want to mention a few things to help him. "Sounding out" is good, but it will not work with all words. Children can pick up clues about the words they are reading from the story, the context of the sentence, or even the pictures. Some stories have rhyming patterns that might help. It might also help them to touch the words with their finger as they read, to better connect the voice sound and the printed word.

Sharing the *We Both Read* books together will engage you and your child in an interactive adventure in reading! It is a fun and easy way to encourage and help your child to read—and a wonderful way to start him off on a lifetime of reading enjoyment!

We Both Read: The Ruby Rose Show

We Both Read® is a trademark of Treasure Bay, Inc.

Published by
Treasure Bay, Inc.
P. O. Box 119
Novato, CA 94948 USA

Printed in Malaysia

Library of Congress Catalog Card Number: 2010921689

Hardcover ISBN: 978-1-60115-245-9
Paperback ISBN: 978-1-60115-246-6

We Both Read® Books
Patent No. 5,957,693

Visit us online at:
www.webothread.com

11-15

WE BOTH READ®

The Ruby Rose Show

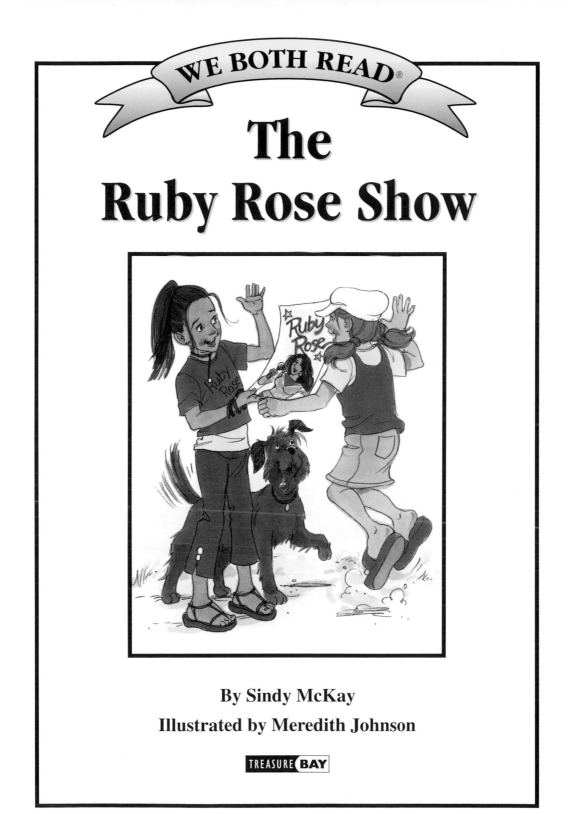

By Sindy McKay

Illustrated by Meredith Johnson

TREASURE **BAY**

 "HURRY UP!!!" Molly said to her big sister, Sarah. "PLEASE! WE'RE GOING TO BE LATE," added Molly's best friend, Abby.

Sarah strolled **slowly** toward the car. "Relax, youngsters. The Ruby Rose **concert** doesn't start for another hour. We have plenty of time."

Sarah had helped Molly and Abby buy the Ruby Rose tickets online. She had even agreed to take them to the **concert**, thought Molly. So why was Sarah moving so **slowly** now?!

3

"The seats are in the 115th row," Sarah reminded the girls as she tossed her jacket in the car. "You might as well just stay home and watch her on TV."

She just doesn't understand, thought Molly. They were about to see the best singer in the whole world—*in person*.

"Did you bring your credit card?" Molly asked her big sister. "We can't pick up our tickets without your credit card."

"I know, I know," Sarah said. "I've got my credit card."

Suddenly, Sarah pulled into a parking lot. "I'm stopping for some gum," she announced. Molly groaned. Why was Sarah torturing them like this?!

As they stood in line to pay for the gum, the couple in front of them noticed that Molly and Abby were wearing Ruby Rose T-shirts. "She's our favorite singer," the man exclaimed with a grin. "Are you going to her concert?"

The girls said yes, they were.

"Well, we don't want you to be late," said the woman. "Would you like to go in front of us?"

Molly and Abby nodded. But Sarah said, "No, thank you."

It took forever, but when they *finally* left the store, Sarah
promised the girls that they would not miss the concert.

They hurried back into the car, and Sarah put the key in the
ignition. She turned it. Nothing happened. She turned it again.
Again nothing happened. Again and again she tried, but the car
would not start.

 Molly and Abby looked at each other. "Oh no!" Molly wailed. "We're going to miss the concert!"

"You won't miss it," said Sarah. "I really, really **promise**."

Sarah calmly called a tow truck to take the car to a repair shop. Then she called for a cab to take them to the show.

After what seemed like a *gajillion* years, the cab **arrived** and the girls all piled in. "Where to?" asked the driver.

"The Ruby Rose concert!" Molly and Abby shouted. "And HURRY!"

By the time they **arrived**, the show had already started.

"Come on! Let's go get our tickets!" said Abby.

Sarah gasped.

"My credit card!" Sarah groaned. "It's in my jacket, and I left the jacket in the car. I'm so sorry, but we'll have to go back and get it."

Abby looked like she was going to cry. Molly, however, just looked determined. "If we go back to the car, we'll miss *everything*," she said. Then she turned and marched up to the ticket booth.

 "Excuse me," Molly said. "My sister left her
credit card in the car. If we promise to bring it to
you later, will you let us in?"

"Sorry. No card—no show."

Now Abby *did* start to cry. Sarah took out her cell phone to call a cab. But Molly was not ready to give up yet.

"Maybe there's another way to get in," she said as she began to walk around the **building**. "Or a door that we can peek through—or *something*!"

Molly came to the side of the **building**. She saw an open door. No one was around. Her heart skipped a beat. Did she dare go inside?

Before Sarah and Abby could stop her, Molly slipped through the door and found herself backstage. People were running around, wearing headsets and holding clipboards. Luckily, they were too busy to notice Molly.

Up ahead, Molly saw the bright lights of the stage and heard singing. Excited, she headed for the stage. At last, she was really going to see Ruby Rose!

Then Molly felt a tap on her back. Oh no! Someone had seen her! Now she would be kicked out! She would *never* see Ruby Rose!

Molly turned slowly, expecting to see a security guard ready to handcuff her and take her off to jail.

"What are you doing back here?" her big sister hissed at her.

Molly breathed a sigh of relief. "I found a way for us to see Ruby Rose," she whispered with a grin.

Abby screamed with joy. "I knew you'd find a way, Molly!"

Sarah was not so happy. "I don't think we should be back here."

Then Molly felt another tap . . .

She turned around, and this time it was a security guard. "Sorry, girls," he said in a gruff voice. "You'll have to come with me."

Now they were in big **trouble**, thought Molly as he led them down the hall.

"Hold on," called a voice from behind them. The girls turned and saw a man and woman waving to the guard.

It was the nice couple from the store where Sarah had stopped for gum.

"Are you in **trouble** too?" Molly asked them.

"Oh, I hope not," said the woman with a smile.

They asked the girls what they were doing backstage, and, in one breath, Molly told them about the car breaking down and the credit card in the jacket and seeing the open door and the security guard finding them and how much they wanted to see Ruby Rose but now would probably end up going to jail instead!

The couple said they did not think anyone was going to end up in jail.

"Come with us," said the man. "We know a way that you can see the show."

They led the girls down one of the backstage hallways. As they walked, the woman told Sarah that she looked about the same age as their own daughter. Sarah smiled, and the man added, "You know, you even look a bit like her when you smile like that!"

 They all went into a big room at the end of the hall. On the wall was a huge TV. On the TV was Ruby Rose, doing her show.

The girls watched the show, clapping and cheering and singing along. They wished that it would go on forever!

When it was over, the nice **couple** asked how they liked it. Abby said it was awesome. Molly said it wasn't the same as seeing Ruby in person, but it was still totally amazing. Sarah said it was better than going to jail, and everyone laughed.

The girls thanked the **couple** over and over again. This was a day they would never forget! Then Sarah said she had better call a cab to take them home.

"Before you go," said the man, "there's someone we'd like you to meet." The couple led the girls back up the hallway and stopped in front of a dressing-room door. On the door was a big star.

Molly and Abby looked at each other and held their breaths. Could it be?

The dressing-room door opened, and Molly's jaw dropped. There stood Ruby Rose!

"Mom! Dad!" she cried. She gave the man and woman each a big hug.

The girls could barely believe what was happening as the nice couple introduced them to their famous daughter. Ruby laughed with them as they told her about their adventures trying to get to the concert.

"After all that," said Ruby, "you deserve to come back and see the concert tomorrow night—in the front row—for free."

Molly and Abby screamed with delight!

"You have done so much for us," Sarah said to
the couple. "I wish there was something we could
do for you!"

They smiled and said they were just happy to help.

Ruby disappeared behind a screen to get the free passes for the next night's show just as the stage manager entered the room.

"Your car is waiting for you, Miss Rose," he said as he tapped Sarah on the shoulder. Sarah turned around, and the stage manager jumped back in surprise.

"I'm sorry," he said. "I thought you were
Ruby. You look just like her from the back."

Ruby's parents laughed. "You *are* the same age and the same height. And you even have the same hair color," said Ruby's mom.

"And don't forget that she has the same smile," added her dad. Then he grinned mischievously at Sarah. "Did you mean it when you said you wished there was something you could do for us, Sarah?"

Sarah nodded, "Of course!"

"Then how would you like to be Ruby for one night?" he asked.

Sarah looked at him in surprise. Molly and Abby were stunned.

He told Sarah that today was Ruby's birthday. Ruby wanted to spend a quiet evening with her parents, eating pizza and bowling, but there was no way to sneak out without her fans following her.

"Would you mind going from the dressing room to the **limo**, pretending to be Ruby?"

Molly and Abby shouted, "Do it, Sarah!"

 "Can Molly and Abby ride in the **limo** too?" asked Sarah.

Ruby's parents said yes. The **limo** would take them all home.

"Then I'll do it."

In an instant, the room was a flurry of activity. The costume lady and the makeup man surrounded Sarah and quickly transformed her into a Ruby Rose impersonator that almost fooled her parents!

Then the security guard led Sarah, Molly, and Abby down the hallway and out the back door, where hundreds of screaming fans were waiting.

"There she is!" a fan shouted. "There's Ruby!"

Soon the fans were all around them. Sarah waved and blew kisses. It was fun to be Ruby Rose for one night!

Sarah blew one last kiss to the fans and entered the limo. Abby followed. Before Molly got in, a fan shouted, "You're so lucky to be Ruby's friend!"

As they drove away, Molly **suddenly** realized just how lucky she really was. Not only was she now Ruby Rose's friend, but she also had the greatest sister in the whole world.

Suddenly, Sarah started to sing a Ruby Rose
song at the top of her lungs. Molly smiled.

Sarah might *look* like Ruby—but she sure
couldn't *sing* like her.

If you liked **The Ruby Rose Show**, here is another
We Both Read® book you are sure to enjoy!

A Pony Named Peanut

Jessica's mother has sent her to spend the
summer with her aunt and uncle in the country.
Jessica doesn't think that living on a farm,
far from a city, will be any fun at all. At first,
she hates life in the country, but then she meets
a special pony that has been rescued from an
animal shelter. Slowly, she begins to think
that this summer might not be so bad after
all. Now, if only that boy, Max, would stop
making fun of her . . .

To see all the We Both Read books that are available,
just go online to **www.webothread.com**.